Francis Robert Beattie

Christ and the cherubim

The ark of the covenant a type of Christ our Saviour

Francis Robert Beattie

Christ and the cherubim
The ark of the covenant a type of Christ our Saviour

ISBN/EAN: 9783337223397

Printed in Europe, USA, Canada, Australia, Japan

Cover: Foto ©Lupo / pixelio.de

More available books at **www.hansebooks.com**

CHRIST AND THE CHERUBIM;

OR,

THE ARK OF THE COVENANT A TYPE OF CHRIST OUR SAVIOUR.

BY

J. M. P. OTTS, LL. D.,

AUTHOR OF "THE LAND WHERE JESUS LIVED," "AT MOTHER'S
KNEE," ETC.

WITH AN INTRODUCTION

BY

FRANCIS R. BEATTIE, B. D., Ph. D., D. D.,

PROFESSOR OF SYSTEMATIC THEOLOGY AND APOLOGETICS IN
THE LOUISVILLE PRESBYTERIAN THEOLOGICAL SEMI-
NARY, LOUISVILLE, KY.

Richmond, Va.:
PRESBYTERIAN COMMITTEE OF PUBLICATION.

PRINTED BY
WHITTET & SHEPPERSON,
RICHMOND, VA.

PREFACE.

THE aim of this little book is to show that the Ark of the Covenant was a type of the man Christ Jesus, the one Mediator between God and men, and the only Saviour of our fallen race, who gave himself a ransom for all, and thereby became the propitiation for our sins, and not for ours only, but also for the whole world. And in doing this it also aims to show that the gospel of love and mercy through a divine Redeemer has always been known from the beginning, being clearly set forth in the types and symbols of all pre-Christian forms of worship, but especially in the Ark of the Covenant, which symbolized Christ our Saviour in his two natures and one person, and in every essential feature of his mediatorial office and redemptive work in the divine scheme of human salvation.

THE AUTHOR.

CONTENTS.

INTRODUCTION.

By Rev. Francis R. Beattie, B. D., Ph. D., D. D.

THE typology of the Sacred Scriptures is an important and useful branch of biblical study. Pursued with sobriety and care, it has both doctrinal use and practical value. At times it has no doubt been pushed to absurd extremes. This was certainly the case with Origen in the Eastern Church, and with Ambrose and Hilary in the Western. The result was the absurdities of the allegorical method of Scripture interpretation, against which sound exegesis must always protest. At other times the nature and value of the study of the types of Scripture have been almost ignored. This is the case with the literal school among the Jews, and with all phases of modern rationalism. Radical higher criticism tends decidedly in the same direction. This is an opposite extreme, which sound exegesis must also firmly condemn.

There is, however, a proper middle view of the

typology of the Scriptures which wisely avoids
both of the extremes above noted, and gives to
the type its rightful place and true meaning.
This view finds its basis in the fact that the
type consists in a real analogy between some
fact in a lower sphere and another fact in a
higher sphere. But other Scripture facts are
also based upon analogy, so that the type has to
be carefully distinguished from these facts.

It must be distinguished from certain forms
of prophecy, where the fact or event is forecast
in the same language-form that describes another fact or event. It must not be confounded
with the allegories of Scripture which prefigure
the fact by means of a representation which is
itself largely, if not entirely, fictitious. Still
less must the type be identified with the symbols of the Bible, which forecast or prefigure
the fact or event merely by a hint of some sort,
more or less definitely given. An example of
each of these scriptural facts may make this
statement clearer. The prediction concerning
the end of the world in connection with that of
the destruction of Jerusalem is prophecy. The

parables of our Lord are, in general, written allegories. Water, with its cleansing and life-giving qualities, is a symbol. The type is illustrated by the Levitical priesthood and by the Mosaic sacrifices, as well as by many other scriptural facts.

It is evidently of the utmost importance to understand the nature of the true scriptural types, and to be able to distinguish them from the allegories and symbols of the word of God. The type presents a fact in a lower sphere as a complete and well-defined representation of some fact in a higher sphere, while the symbol is a mere sign, and the allegory a more or less fictitious representation of the fact or truth. The type is real and definite in its nature, so that what it means in reference to its antitype can be readily understood. The type as a sign is real and indefinite, and the antitype is clearly seen to be real also over against the type in the Scriptures.

Dr. Otts is clearly right in ascribing a typical significance to the Ark of the Covenant, and he has rendered the student of the Bible valuable service in unfolding its interpretation in relation to the person and saving work of our Lord Jesus Christ. He has also taken safe middle ground in working out the typical meaning of the ark; and although some readers may not agree with him in all the details of his excellent and suggestive exposition, yet all who peruse it must frankly admit that the grand outline sketched in these interesting pages is alike scriptural and devout.

We have always been convinced that the sober and devout study of the types of Scripture renders an important service in showing the intimate connection between the Old Testament and the New. This fact binds the two Testaments firmly and closely together. The force of this fact is especially seen in the case of the Messianic types. The result of the careful study of such types is to show the unity and harmony of the several parts of the Sacred Scriptures, and to reveal very clearly the fact that one divine mind must have presided over the production of both Testaments. This is a matter of the highest value at the present day.

No one can read what Dr. Otts has written about a single important typical object in the Old Testament without having his faith in the divine origin and inspiration of the Scriptures greatly confirmed. Against modern naturalistic views of the origin and nature of the Scriptures this is a very valuable apologetic service which this volume renders.

In particular, we have always felt that the study of the entire tabernacle and its gospel significance is well worthy the careful attention of modern biblical scholars. To understand the meaning of the tabernacle, with its court, its holy place and its holy of holies, to be able to interpret the furniture of its various sections, such as the brazen altar and laver of the court, the shewbread, candlestick, and altar of incense in the holy place, and the ark of the testimony and other things within the holy of holies, and to see the significance of the various sacrifices and offerings, especially those of the Day of Atonement, is of the highest value in giving us a clear and definite view of the saving doctrines, of the grace of God in Jesus Christ. The Epistle to the Hebrews is the inspired key to the typology of the tabernacle.

We do well to study carefully the Epistle to the Romans in order to obtain clear and comprehensive views of the great doctrines of the grace of God in the salvation of sinners, and to secure a right understanding of justification and sanctification in their relations to each other in the recovery of the sinner both from the guilt and pollution of sin. Still, we are convinced that it will be found very helpful to set the Epistle to the Hebrews beside that to the Romans in our study of the doctrines of grace from the view-point of the scriptural basis. In Hebrews we will find the same doctrines of grace set forth in a new and somewhat different form, and with very special reference to the Old Testament economy of type and symbol. Such study will show the full meaning of the Old Testament and reveal the gospel under the Mosaic law; and at the same time it will illumine with concrete reality what is in abstract didactic form stated in Romans. The reading of what Dr. Otts has written on one

aspect of this wide theme ought to whet the
appetite of the reader to pursue the same line
of inquiry all through the Epistle to the Hebrews. We cannot refrain from adding that
Dr. Otts himself could well give us something
further along the line we are now suggesting,
and we hope that he may do so.

Another thing deserves notice in connection
with the study of typology. Its study rever-
ently pursued tends to conserve and foster evangelical views of Scripture truth. From the
nature of the case this is evident, because it is
a severely scriptural line of inquiry when
rightly pursued. The history of the religious
life of the church points to the same conclu-
sion. Augustine opposed the allegorical ex-
travagances of Ambrose and Hilary, and at
the same time he adopted and applied a sober
view of the types of Scripture. We all know
how deep and devout was the religious experience of the sage and saint of Hippo. Many
of the Reformers distinguished carefully between the types of Scripture and its allegories
and symbols, and made excellent use of the

types in expounding the doctrines of grace. The Pietists, too, a little later, cultivated the study of typology diligently in connection with their deep and devout religious life and activity. In like manner we observe, side by side with the revival of religion which occurred in many quarters about the beginning of this century, a renewed interest in the study of typology. It seems quite evident, therefore, that the right study of the types of Sacred Scriptures conduces to evangelical views of the doctrines of grace, and proves eminently helpful to a genuine and spiritual religious experience.

It is perhaps in this connection that this book from the able pen of Dr. Otts has its chief value and importance. The book is entirely evangelical in its general doctrinal views, and is decidedly spiritual and elevating in its tone. This was to be expected when a sound position was taken in regard to the typology of the Scriptures. Hence, we observe that in regard to the person of our Lord as the God-man, in regard to the nature of his sacrificial work for us, and in regard to the fulness and gracious

nature of the redemption which we have in
Jesus Christ, this book is plain, simple and
scriptural.   This is a refreshing feature of what
Dr. Otts has given for our perusal, especially
at the present day, when naturalistic ideas of
scriptural doctrine and religious life are so
prevalent.   No one can read these pages without edification and comfort.

The book, therefore, has our hearty commen-
dation.   We hope that it may be widely circu-
lated and find many readers.   Above all, may
God's blessing go with its message of instruc-
tion and edification.

I.

THE Ark of the Covenant was the most sacred and significant of all the holy things that were used in the typical worship of the old dispensation. It was made according to a divine pattern that was shown Moses in the Mount, and for a specific purpose that was divinely revealed. It was a double chest, one of wood inclosed in one of gold. The wooden one was so thoroughly incased, within and without, in the golden one, that the ark, in its external appearance, seemed to the eye to be a single chest of solid gold. It was two and a half cubits long, and a cubit and a half in breadth and height. There was a lid of gold on the top of it, and, surrounding it, a crown of gold, and fitting into this crown there was on the lid a mercy-seat of solid gold, the two ends of which were beaten out and fashioned

2   17

into cherubim. The faces of the cherubim were turned toward one another, looking down upon the mercy-seat, which was covered with their outstretched wings. Over the mercy-seat, between the cherubim, there was what the later Jews called the Shechinah, a visible manifestation of the divine presence in which "God communed with his people of all things concerning which he gave them commandments." At each of the four corners there was a ring of solid gold, and through these rings were inserted two staves, one on each side, by which the ark was borne and moved from place to place. These staves were of acacia wood, overlaid with gold. They were never taken out of the rings, showing that this sacred vessel was always kept in readiness to be moved on a moment's notice, if occasion should arise. The ark contained the two unbroken tables of stone, on which were written, by the finger of God, the ten commandments of the moral law. It seems that these two tables were the only things that were *inside* this holy vessel. (1 Kings viii. 9.) Aaron's rod that budded, and a golden pot of manna, and, perhaps, some other very sacred things, were laid up *before the ark* in the holy of holies in the tabernacle and in the temple. In its holy place, the ark was the centre of the tabernacle and temple service, around which all typical rites and ceremonies of worship revolved.

This sacred chest went before the children of Israel, borne by the Kohathites in the centre of the army, on their marches through the wilderness to Canaan. After the conquest of the land the tabernacle was set up at Shiloh, where it was stationary for three hundred years as the dwelling-place of the ark. In the days of Eli this sacred vessel was taken out of the tabernacle and borne by his wicked sons, Hophni and Phinehas, into battle with the Philistines, into whose hands it fell in a disastrous defeat of Israel, and by whom it was borne away in proud triumph to the temple of their great idol. But the Philistines, moved by the heavy affliction of God upon themselves and their idol, returned it to the Israelites in a most signal manner. It was then lodged at Kirjath-Jearim, where it remained until the days of David, who, when he found himself firmly seated on the throne, built for it a new tabernacle on Mount Zion. When Solomon came to the throne he built the glorious temple on Mount Moriah, to which the ark was transferred from David's tabernacle, and in which it found its last resting-place on earth.

No one knows certainly what finally became of this, the most sacred of all the holy things used in the tabernacle and temple worship. It does not seem that it was carried to Babylon, for it is not mentioned in the account of the destruction of Solomon's temple, nor is it enumerated in the list of the holy things which were restored on the return from the Babylonian captivity. Some suppose that, in the stormy days just preceding the captivity, it may have been hidden in some secret subterranean chamber in the bosom of Mount Moriah, where it still remains, and that it may yet be found and be brought forth from its hiding-place at some future day as a witness from the tomb of dead centuries to the historical verity of the biblical record.

The Jews have a tradition that the ark was miraculously translated to heaven when Nebuchadnezzar captured the temple, and that it will be restored to earth by the Messiah when he comes. We believe that Christ is the great archetype of all that was prefigured and typified in the Ark of the Covenant, and that in his incarnation the ark was truly restored to earth in his life, which was the fulfilment of all that it signified. John, in his apocalyptic vision, saw the Ark of Testimony in the temple of God in heaven. (Rev. xi. 19.) This may mean that the ark is now in the temple of God in heaven, in the exalted person of Christ, the great archetype, and that it will be restored to earth when he shall return in great glory to judge men.

Why was this sacred chest called the Ark of the Covenant? There must have been a covenant of which it was, in its typical significance, the exponent and seal. But what covenant? It was, to begin with, the covenant of God with

the children of Israel as his chosen and peculiar people, of whom the Messiah, as typified
in the ark, should be born ; but this covenant,
in its widest scope, was not limited to Israel.
It embraced all mankind, because the promised
Messiah of the Jews, when born, would be the
Saviour of the fallen world. " Salvation is of
the Jews." (John iv. 22.) But salvation is not
for the Jews only, but for the whole world. It
was promised in the covenant made with Abraham that in his seed all the families of all the
nations of the whole earth should be blessed.
The covenant with Abraham and the children
of Israel had a limitizing scope, focalizing the
promise of the coming Messiah to a chosen
people ; then to a chosen nation of the chosen
people ; then to a chosen tribe of the chosen
nation, and, finally, to a chosen family of the
chosen tribe. But while there was this descending and limitizing element in the covenant
made with the chosen people, there was at the
same time a world-wide scope in its intentions
and benefits, embracing all families of all nations in its ever-expanding provisions. Hence,

the great commission of the Christian dispensation is, "Go ye into all the world and preach
my gospel in all nations, and to every creature." Then the Ark of the Covenant was, in
the wide scope of its typical significance, the
exponent and seal of the covenant of salvation
between God and men.

What is involved in this covenant? In our
search for the true answer to this question we
begin with the inquiry, What is a covenant?
The Child's Catechism answers, in simplest
words, "an agreement between two or more
persons." A contract may be defined in precisely the same words. But a contract and a
covenant are not precisely the same thing.
The word "covenant" is derived from *con* and
venire, to come together, and the word "contract" from *con* and *trahere*, to draw together.
In both there are mutual obligations growing
out of the relations existing between the persons or parties concerned, but there is a differ-
ence in the mode in which the relations were
established. In a contract the relations and
their obligations are created by the conscious

and voluntary acts of the persons involved; but in a covenant the relations may be natural and spontaneous, and, in such cases, the mutual obligations would be inevitable.

A man and a woman are drawn together in the contract of marriage; but being drawn together in the contract of marriage, there naturally and spontaneously springs up a covenant between them as possible parents and whatever children may be born to them as the fruit of their marriage. Thus, in marriage there arises, naturally and spontaneously, a covenant between husband and wife as possible parents and the children not yet born, a covenant in which one of the parties has not yet come into existence. In the contract of marriage there is involved a covenant which binds the parents to give to the children that may be born to them the best possible opportunity in life, and which also obligates the children when born, as they come to years of discretion, to give to their parents filial reverence and obedience. Thus parents and children come together, naturally and inevitably, under the mutual obligations of a covenant that began to exist before the children were born.

There is, in the nature of things, a similar covenant between God and men involved in the very act of creation. In creation God and man came together in the relations of a covenant which requires God, as Creator, to give to man, his creature, the very best possible opportunity in life, and which requires man, as creature, to give to God, his Creator, the perfect obedience and worship of his life. This covenant is involved, by the eternal principle of justice, in every act of creation.

Then, the first covenant of salvation between God and men was the covenant of creation, made on the eternal foundation of absolute and immutable justice. It is commonly called the covenant of works, because the continuance of God's favor to man was conditioned on his perfect obedience to the law of justice in all the works of his life.

Under this covenant man was placed on probation in the garden of Eden. The mutual obligations of eternal justice in this covenant demanded that man should obey God, and that God should give him eternal life on the condition of his perfect obedience to his law. We call this the covenant of justice in creation.

In this covenant man failed and fell by an act of voluntary disobedience. In the fall eternal justice obligated man to suffer, and God to inflict upon him the penalty of eternal death, unless there should be found a way consistent with eternal justice to evade this penalty.

Man by his sin was justly condemned to the penalty of eternal death; and if he had been left to himself his case would have been helpless and hopeless. But God in his infinite wisdom found a way for human salvation by making a provision for mercy in a new covenant of redemption. A competent Redeemer was provided for man, who, as his accepted substitute, by his own perfect obedience even unto death, has made absolute satisfaction to violated justice, and thus on the crown of fulfilled justice has established a mercy-seat, the throne of grace.

This new covenant of redemption through

mercy does not abrogate the old covenant of creation that was grounded in justice, but adds to it a new provision for salvation on the condition of faith in the Redeemer, involving repentance for sin and an endeavor towards a life of new obedience.

The new covenant is commonly called the covenant of grace; but we prefer to call it, at least in this present discussion, the covenant of mercy in redemption, and thus to contrast it with the covenant of justice in creation. Thus the holy God of heaven and the sinful men of earth come together, or may come together, in a new way of life in a covenant of mercy unto redemption.

This, of course, involves the old-fashioned doctrine of man's fall by sin and of his redemption by the blood of the atonement of a Saviour who died for him as his sacrificial substitute on earth. If any object, we can only answer this is what the Bible teaches. The Bible is from beginning to end the inspired history of human redemption. It begins with a condensed account of the creation of man, and of his proba-

tion under the law of justice in the covenant of
his creation, and tells how he fell into sin and
incurred the just penalty of eternal death, in
order that the necessity and nature of redemption might be seen and comprehended, and
thus the story of the gospel plan of salvation
begins in Genesis and runs through the entire
book as an unbroken chain, holding all dispensations in harmony and continuity. It is the
divine history of human redemption through
Jesus Christ, who, by his sacrificial death in
obedience unto justice, has become the beginning of the grace in mercy, and the end of the
law in justice, to every one who believeth in
him. All this was clearly revealed and illustrated in the types and symbols of the worship
of the old dispensation; and the Ark of the
Covenant, the central type around which all
the typical acts of worship revolved, was the
great type of Christ our Saviour in the covenant of redemption.

II.

THE ARK, IN ALL ITS PARTS AND CON-
TENTS. A TYPE OF CHRIST IN HIS PER-
SON AND REDEMPTIVE WORK.

THE Ark of the Covenant, as a type of Christ, was, in its materials and form, a type of the two natures in the one person of the Man Christ Jesus. It was composed of two boxes, one of wood and the other of gold, so united that the two together formed but one chest. The perfect wood of the inner box was a type of Christ's perfect human nature, and the precious metal of the outer box was a type of his perfect divine nature. The two boxes, the wooden one incased within the golden one, were so blended and wrought together that they constituted but one thing, the Ark of the Covenant, in the materials and form of which we find a perfect type of the two natures in the one person of the Man Christ Jesus. The inner wooden box did not have a wooden cover over it, but was covered by the lid of the outer box, which was of solid gold. This typified the fact that the human nature in Christ is not coequal with his divine nature. The human is finite, and the divine infinite. In the incarnation the human became one with the divine, but not equal to it. The river flowing into the sea becomes one with it, but never fills it, nor freshens the salt waters of the boundless ocean, but the tide, going up the river, fills it to overflowing, and imparts to its waters the saltness of the sea. So in Christ, our Saviour, humanity was deified and made more than human, but not infinite, and divinity was humanized, but not made finite. Thus the two natures were so united in him as to constitute one person, the Man Christ Jesus, who is the one mediator between God and men.

The Ark of the Covenant contained, shut up in its bosom, the two unbroken tables of stone on which was written the moral law in ten commandments, inscribed by the finger of God. It contained nothing else. (2 Chron. vi. 10.) Those tables were so inclosed in the ark under the golden lid, on which the mercy-seat rested, that they could not be taken out without removing the mercy-seat and breaking open the holy chest. In this we find a type of Christ's perfect obedience to the moral law, by which he has made full satisfaction to all the demands of justice against the sinner, and so shut up the law within himself by his own perfect obedience. Thus he has become the end of the law to every one who believeth in him, because, as our Saviour, he has completed and closed the covenant of justice made in creation, and prepared, on the top of fulfilled justice, the throne of grace, on which mercy reigns in the covenant of redemption.

The two tables of the law which were inclosed in the ark were not the first ones on which God wrote the ten commandments. Those tables Moses dashed down upon the ground when, descending from the mount, he found the children of Israel worshipping the golden calf which Aaron had made; and they were broken in pieces and left in fragments upon the earth, typifying the power of the broken law unto condemnation against all who do not accept Christ as their Saviour in the covenant of redemption. Those broken tables are the symbols of the law as broken by the disobedience of man in the covenant of justice which was made with him in his creation. All men are under the law. Those in Christ are under the unbroken tables of the law, that is, under the law as fulfilled by him, and so they are delivered from its curse. Those who are out of Christ, living in the world without Christ, are under the broken law, and so they are under its curse. "For as many as are of the works of the law are under the curse: for it is written, Cursed is every one that continueth not in all things which are written in the book of the law to do them." But it is also written, "Christ hath redeemed us from the curse of the law, being made a curse for us."

The ark, properly speaking, consisted of the holy chest which contained the law, sealed up in it. That chest constituted the foundation on which the mercy-seat, and all that belonged to it, rested. In all this the mediatorial person and redemptive work of Christ our Saviour was typified ; and the glorious fact was taught that Christ Jesus, by the blood of his vicarious atonement, has closed the covenant of justice, and made it the foundation for the new covenant of mercy.

The place for the mercy-seat was on the top of the golden lid of the chest that contained, shut up in its bosom, the unbroken tables of the law. It was not the lid itself, but a separate piece of solid gold fitting in the golden crown around the lid. This teaches that it is only out of the finished and crowned work of justice that mercy can shine forth for the salvation of sinners. It is only when mercy and truth meet together that righteousness and peace can kiss each other.

The great problem of human salvation is to find a way in which God can be just while justifying the unjust. The gospel is the only solution : "God so loved the world that he gave his only begotten Son, that whosoever believeth in him should not perish, but have everlasting life." This gospel was written in

3

all the types of the worship of the old dispensation.   It was typified in all the parts and
contents of the ark ; and the mercy-seat, on
the top of fulfilled justice, was a type of Christ
our Saviour in the completion of his redemptive work, by which he has become "the propitiation for our sins, and not for ours only,
but also for the sins of the whole world."

Over the mercy-seat, between the cherubim,
there was a visible manifestation of the presence of God with his people, in which, in some
mysterious way, he met and " communed with
them of all things concerning which he gave
them commandments."   As to its appearance,
we infer, from scriptural and Talmudic allu-
sions to it, that it was a brilliant light envel-
oped in a cloud of smoke, and so concealed
that the cloud alone was, for the most part,
visible, but, on special occasions, the glory of it
appeared as a flame in a luminous cloud.   The
post-biblical Jews named this visible manifestation of the divine presence over the mercy-
seat the Shechinah.   This name is not found
in the Bible, but the thing it designates is

clearly and frequently referred to. It was first used in the Targums, especially by Onkelos and Jonathan, to avoid ascribing corporeity to God in his presence among men. Where the Hebrew, in Exodus xxv. 8, reads, "Let them make me a sanctuary, that I may dwell among them," Onkelos has, "that my Shechinah may dwell among them." And in the description of the dedication of the temple, where the Hebrew, in 1 Kings viii. 13, makes Solomon say, "I have built thee a house to dwell in, a settled place for thee to abide in forever," the Targum of Jonathan reads, "I have built the house of the sanctuary for the house of the Shechinah forever."

We adopt this title, not from the superstitious motive that prompted the Jews to invent it, but because it is convenient and expressive, and because it denotes the fact that, even in the conviction of the Talmudic Jews, the visible manifestation of the divine presence over the ark was the significant thing that gave vitality and worth to the worship of the tabernacle and temple.

The Shechinah over the mercy-seat on the

ark had a special typical significance, showing that it is only in and through Christ, as typified in the ark, that God can dwell among men.

There was no ark in the second temple, and consequently no Shechinah. The Jews lamented this as a mark of divine favor wanting to that temple, and they expected the restoration of the Shechinah at the coming of the Messiah. Jonathan paraphrases Hag. i. 8 thus: "I will cause my Shechinah to dwell in it (the second temple) in glory." Christ came in person to the second temple. In it he was presented to the Lord in his infancy, and he ministered in it, claiming it as his Father's house, and he cleansed it from human pollution at the beginning and end of his earthly ministry. Thus he conferred upon it, by his real presence in it, a greater glory than that of the first temple, in which he typically dwelt in the Ark of the Covenant in its most holy place. But the type was more fully realized in its great antitype, in that "the Word was made flesh and dwelt among men, full of grace and truth," and men beheld his glory, "as the glory of the only begotten of the Father." And the Shechinah, or rather the reality of which it was the type, is still with the church on earth in the perpetual fulfilment of the promise, "Lo, I am with you alway, even unto the end of the world."

III.

THE CHERUBIM ON THE MERCY-SEAT A TYPE OF THE ETERNAL LIFE OF THE REDEEMED.

BOTH ends of the mercy-seat were beaten out and fashioned into cherubim. We can never know exactly what was the form of these mystic figures. They had faces and wings, but otherwise their form and shape are not clearly described. Those seen by Ezekiel in vision had the form of composite creatures, of which the man, lion, ox and eagle were the elements. The peculiar cherubic form is, and perhaps will always remain, an impenetrable mystery. But this we know, whatever may have been their shape and form, they were not images of persons or things in heaven or on earth; for all such images were expressly prohibited by the law contained in the ark under them. They were types, and types are not images of things, but symbols of thought. As the ark, in all its parts and contents, was a type

38

of Christ our Saviour, it follows the cherubim on the mercy-seat must have been typical of some great truth pertaining to human salvation.

It could not be that they were designed, as some have thought, to represent the angels as bending over the mercy-seat, "desirous of looking into the mystery of human redemption," because they were themselves a part of the very mercy-seat itself, being the two ends of it beaten out and fashioned into mystic figures. They could no more be images of glorified saints than of angels that never fell.

As they were a part of the very mercy-seat itself, it seems that they must have been designed to typify the full result of the mercy of God towards men through Christ our Saviour, whose person and redemptive work were typified in the ark which they overshadowed with their outstretched wings. That result is the deliverance from the death of sin and the gift of eternal life. "The wages of sin is death; but the gift of God is eternal life through Jesus Christ our Lord." (Rom. vi. 23.)

The ark, in all that was under the mercy-seat,

typified Christ in all that he has done to take
away the death-penalty of sin. By his perfect
obedience, even unto death, he has closed the
covenant of justice under which the fallen race
is lost and doomed to eternal death. The
mercy-seat on the ark typified the result of all
that Christ our Saviour has done in order to
open for us the covenant of mercy in redemption
unto eternal life. And hence the cherubim,
arising out of the very mercy-seat itself, symbolized the eternal life of the redeemed, which
is the gift of God through Jesus Christ our
Lord. The cherubim were not images of the
saints in heaven, but of the eternal life itself
which redeemed men live in glory.

The cherubim are everywhere in Scripture
spoken of as "the living creatures," showing that
life itself is the central thought in their typical
signification. The life they represent is life
from death—the life of redemption—life that
had been forfeited under justice but restored
through mercy—that eternal life which is the
gift of God through Jesus Christ the Redeemer
and Saviour of men.

We cannot reiterate it too often, that the cherubim were not images of the glorified forms of men, but mystic figures, that symbolized the fulness and felicity of the eternal life of the redeemed human souls in the glory of heaven. Jesus our Redeemer and Saviour is spoken of as the Lamb of God that taketh away the sin of the world, and John, in his apocalyptic vision, saw him on the throne in heaven as the Lamb that had been slain from the foundation of the world. This does not warrant us to expect to find Jesus in heaven in the shape and form of a lamb; but we will find in him the reality of all that of which the sacrificial lamb was the type and symbol. Just so, we are not to expect to find the saints in heaven, who have been redeemed from sin through the grace of Christ, in the shape and form of the cherubim that were on the mercy-seat of the ark, or of the cherubim that appeared in vision to Ezekiel and John, but we will find in their eternal life in heaven all the ineffable greatness and glory that those cherubim typically represented.

Any one who will carefully read what is said

of the cherubim in the Book of Ezekiel, and compare it with what is said of the living creatures in the Book of Revelation, cannot fail to see that the living creatures and the cherubim are the same, and that the vision of the prophet was substantially the same as that of the apostle. It was in both instances a vision of the throne of God in the kingdom of redemption. The living creatures of Revelation—not $\theta\eta\rho\iota\alpha$, but $\zeta\hat{\omega}\alpha$—are undoubtedly identical with the cherubim of Ezekiel's vision. The cherubim stood around and supported the throne of redemption, and were associated around the Lamb with the four and twenty elders and the hosts of the redeemed, with whom they joined in singing the new song of redemption, which none but those redeemed by the blood of Christ, as the Lamb slain from the foundation of the world, can sing. (Ezek. i. and Rev. iv.) This settles the question. The cherubim on the mercy-seat and those seen by Ezekiel and John, and cherubim wherever they are mentioned in Scripture, are identical, and they typically represent the eternal life of the redeemed in heaven. They symbolize the eternal life of that innumerable host that are saved by Christ our Redeemer out of every nation and kindred and tribe and tongue of earth.

We shall not attempt to interpret the symbolic meaning of their composite forms and diverse faces, and of their wings that were full of eyes, and of the wheels that revolved within wheels, except to say, in general terms, that all these characteristics typified the might and majesty, the wisdom and glory, and the fulness and felicity of the eternal life of the redeemed. We know not in detail what that life shall be, and so it cannot be expressed in words nor represented to our senses in symbols that can now be fully unfolded and comprehended. And all this is in full accord with the uniform teaching of Holy Scripture, that the life that is eternal is spiritual, and can be only spiritually discerned. It can be represented to us now only as shadows in types and symbols. "Eye hath not seen, nor ear heard, neither have entered into the heart of man, the things which God hath prepared for them that love him." There is more glory in the eternal life of the redeemed in heaven than the highest imagination of earth can conceive. This does not mean that the blessings of the eternal life are all future, but that they are spiritual, and therefore they cannot now be adequately represented to the senses of our physical perception. All that we can now say is, "Beloved, now are we the sons of God, and it doth not yet appear what we shall be; but we know that when he shall appear we shall be like him; for we shall see him as he is." When we shall see Christ our Saviour in all the fulness in which the Ark of the Covenant of our salvation typified him, then shall we appear in all the fulness of that eternal life that was typified in the cherubim on the mercy-seat. And in the meantime, while we wait in faith for the day of our full redemption, we know that we dwell in him, and he in us, because he hath given us of his Spirit. And we have seen and do testify that the Father hath sent the Son to be the Saviour of the world. "And we know that the Son of God is come, and hath given us an understanding, that we know him that is true, even his Son Jesus Christ. This is the true God and eternal life."

IV.

WHEN man fell, God did not forsake the earth and deliver it over to the undisputed dominion of Satan, and leave man to perish in eternal death under the penalty of justice incurred by his disobedience to the law of the covenant of his creation. He began the work of redemption immediately, with the promise that " the seed of the woman should bruise the head of the serpent." In the evening of that fatal day Adam and Eve " heard the voice of the Lord God *walking* in the garden." It was not the sound of speech, but the sound of a footfall, they heard. In some way they became conscious that the Lord God was approaching them. The voice of the Lord God was, doubtless, the Eternal Word, the second person in the adorable Trinity, which afterwards was made flesh and dwelt' among men.

45

Thus, immediately on the heels of the fall, Christ our Saviour appeared on earth to begin the work of human redemption. God could no longer save man by dealing with him in the garden of Eden, where he was under the law of justice in the covenant of his creation. In the garden of Eden he could do nothing for man except to inflict upon him the penalty of eternal death, which his disobedience justly deserved. The garden of Eden was the domain of the covenant of creation, and was under the dominion of absolute justice as the law of that covenant. So long as man remained in it after his fall he was under the law of the covenant of his creation, and, consequently, under the sentence of violated justice. Under that law he was condemned to eternal death, that is, to endless life in sin and its misery.

The garden of Eden, after the fall of man, was no longer the paradise of life and the joys of life, but was the domain of death and the abode of despair. Not in wrath, but in love, God drove fallen man out of the garden of Eden, because, if he had been left in it after his fall, he would have remained, by the covenant of his creation, under the law of justice, and thus, by the very act of his remaining, he would have put forth his hand and taken of the tree of life, and, by eating thereof, would have lived on forever in the endless death of sin. He was taken out of the garden, which, in consequence of his sin, had become the dominion of death, in order that he might be transferred from the dominion of justice in the covenant of his creation and placed under the law of mercy in the new covenant of redemption. This was the only way in which it was possible for God to rescue the fallen race and save men from the penalty of eternal death, that is, endless life in the misery of sin. When driven out of the garden of Eden, mercy met fallen man at the gate as he fled from justice, and received him under the new covenant of redemption.

This new covenant required a new system of worship. Henceforth man is to be saved, not by his own obedience to the law of justice, but by his faith in the person and mediation of a Saviour who would come, as the seed of the

woman, to bruise the head of the serpent. By
thus satisfying the demands of justice, Christ
has shut the gate of death; and he has opened
the door of life by providing for sinful men "a
new and living way" of reconciliation and com-
munion with God. This new relation of man
to God in the covenant of redemption demanded a new form of worship, having symbols and ceremonies that set forth the doctrine
of human redemption by the sacrificial atonement of a living Redeemer.

Accordingly, we find that an altar was dedi-
cated just outside of the gate of the garden of
Eden, and the sacrifice of animals was divinely
appointed as a didactic form of worship, typifying the great sacrifice that the promised Redeemer would make of himself for man in order
that he might be the Saviour of our lost race.

It is quite evident that there was, from the
very beginning, an altar of worship, and also a
service of sacrifices and offerings. The altar
for blood sacrifice stands on the very threshold
of the history of man after the fall. Inspiration does not give an account of the origin of

this mode of worship, but, as it is introduced to our notice at the very beginning of human history as a mode of worship divinely approved, we must suppose that it originated as a divine institution. We have a hint as to the divine origin and date of this primitive institution in the fact recorded in Gen. iii. 21, that "the Lord God made coats of skin and clothed" Adam and Eve in them immediately after the fall. The best theologians suppose that the skins were taken from animals that were offered in sacrifice. When, in the process of time, or in the end of the days, perhaps on the Sabbath, at the end of the week days, Cain and Abel *brought* their offerings, they must have come to a certain place where it was customary to worship. From this we infer that there was a standing altar that was the holy trysting place between Jehovah and his worshippers. This is implied in the expression that they *brought their offerings unto the Lord.*

It also seems that there was, at the very beginning, in connection with the altar, an Ark of the Covenant, or something possessing its

4

essential parts, and similar to it in use. We
read, in Genesis iii. 24 : "So he drove out the
man; and he placed at the east of the garden
òf Eden cherubim, and a flaming sword which
turned every way, *to keep the way of the tree of
life.*" There were cherubim, more than one
of them, but only *one* thing that was like a
flaming sword which turned every way. This
does not fall in with the idea which many hold,
that the gate of lost Eden was guarded by a
number of cherubim, armed with flaming
swords, to bar the way of access to the tree of
life. The flaming sword, whatever it was, was
not in the hands of the cherubim; it was self-
moving, turning in every direction. There is
no reason to believe that the cherubim were
living creatures at all. It is true that Ezekiel
and John described the cherubim which they
saw as living creatures of wonderful form and
motion, but what they saw were symbolic
figures seen in prophetic vision, mere pictures
formed in an inspired imagination; and there
is no reason to suppose that there ever existed
in actual life, in heaven or on earth, any such

beings. The cherubim at the east of the garden of Eden may have been lifeless, typical forms like the golden cherubim on the mercy-seat and the other cherubic forms that were represented in the tabernacle and temple. And further, there is no reason to believe that "the flaming sword which turned every way" was a sword at all. Common sense suggests that it was a flame like unto the gleam of a sword flashing in the sunlight and turning every way. The flame had self-motion, and was like a blaze of fire moved by the wind, turning it in all directions. Why may it not have been the original Shechinah blazing between the cherubim and turning itself in first one direction and then another? Here, then, in all probability, we find the cherubim which were found on the mercy-seat of the Ark of the Covenant, and between them the luminous cloud, sometimes flashing out as a brilliant light, which is everywhere the symbol of the divine presence, before whom alone it was lawful to offer sacrifices in worship. Dr. Kurtz has clearly shown in his *Sacred History* that it was lawful to

erect an altar and to offer sacrifices only where
the Shechinah appeared as the symbol of the
presence of the Lord, to whom the sacrifice was
offered. It was lawful to erect a permanent
altar for sacrifices only where the ark had its
dwelling-place, or where the Shechinah, which
was the glory of the ark, was permanently
manifested; but whenever the Lord appeared
to an individual *elsewhere*, sacrifices could be
offered in that spot also, for his presence in it
made it, for the time being, a Bethel, and rendered it a lawful place for sacrifices. But
when his immediate presence was withdrawn
from the spot, all authority to offer sacrifices in
it ceased. Then we conclude that it was the
presence of the cherubim and the Shechinah
dwelling between them, like a flaming sword
turning in all directions, that consecrated the
original altar on the very threshold of redemption, on which Adam and Eve and their children offered sacrifices.

Those cherubim and the Shechinah between
them were the prototype of the Ark of the
Covenant, and the original type of Christ our

Saviour, who, from the beginning, appeared unto men as the source and medium of divine mercy and salvation in the new covenant of redemption.

The cherubim and the flaming sword were appointed "to keep the way of the tree of life." This does not mean, as many have supposed, to block up the way of access, but *to keep open* a proper way of approach to it. The Hebrew word *shamar* (שָׁמַר) means to preserve and maintain in good condition. It is the same word that is used in Gen. ii. 15, where it is said that man was put in the garden of Eden "to dress and *keep it.*" And we are to note that it was not the tree of life itself, but *the way* of the tree of life, that was to be kept. This means that it was not to be barred, but preserved and kept open.

There is no difficulty in this interpretation if we only remember that man was under the law of justice in the covenant of his creation, and under that law the tree of justice, which, before the fall, was to him the tree of life, had become to him, in his fall, the tree of spiritual

death ; and if man, in his fallen condition, had
eaten of the fruit of the tree of justice, he would
have lived forever in the eternal death of an
endless life in sin and its misery.   God in justice might have left fallen man in the garden of
Eden, in the covenant of creation, under the
doom of justice ; there, what would have been
to him the tree of life if he had obeyed, had
become to him, in his accomplished disobedience, the tree of endless death in his naturally immortal existence.   Henceforth, not the
tree of justice in the covenant of creation, but
the tree of mercy in the covenant of redemption, is the tree of life for fallen man.   The
cherubim, and the flame like a sword between
them, were appointed, not *to close*, but to keep
open, the way of this tree of life.   The covenant of redemption is not a covenant unto
death, but a covenant unto eternal life, as the
gift of God through Jesus Christ, our Lord and
Saviour.   Christ Jesus, by the blood of the
atonement of his sacrificial death, has closed
the covenant of creation, in which the law of
justice was supreme, and opened the covenant

of redemption, in which the law of mercy is enthroned on the crown of satisfied justice, and he has thus become the tree of life and the end of the law to every one that believeth in him. This fact was made known to the race immediately after the fall, and just outside the gate of the garden of Eden a system of worship was instituted with didactic symbols and types that taught in fulness all the fundamental doctrines of the gospel as we now possess them.

It has been thought by some that Moses caught the idea of the ark and the cherubim from the Egyptians, and that they in turn had caught the idea from the Babylonians and Persians. But there was, no doubt, a protevangelium preached at the gate of paradise; and a typical form of worship was then instituted, which was the common mode among men before the flood, and which prevailed up to the dispersion of families after the flood; and so we are not to be surprised at finding many religious symbols in pagan worship similar to those that were in use among the ancient Jews; and the fact that sacred chests or cistae similar to the

Mosaic ark, and many figures of composite
beings with wings and faces similar to cherubim, are found to have been common in the
worship of all eastern nations, does not argue
that Moses derived his ideas from Egypt or
any other pagan source, but rather that tradi-
tions and reminiscences of the protevangel and
the primitive forms of worship have been carried into all nations of the earth, but were
more fully conserved in some than in others.
The remarkable similarity that has been found
to prevail in some of the ancient eastern sacred
rites and symbols of worship and the Mosaic
institutions is to be attributed to the fact that
they had a common origin in the primitive
forms of worship that were instituted just outside the gate of the garden of Eden, where
Christ first made himself known to men as the
Saviour of our fallen world. A true knowledge of human history does not teach that
Christianity originated as an evolution from
paganism, but that paganism, in all its multitu-
dinous forms, originated in a downward and di-
vergent devolution from the primitive truths of

Christianity, which were revealed to man immediately after the fall, and which all mankind held in common up to the time when the dispersion of families began. There were two dispersions of families, one before and one after the flood. All families which had fallen away prior to the flood from the knowledge and worship of the true God were destroyed in the deluge, and the race had a new start in religious knowledge and life in the family of Noah; and hence, the divergences in language and religion which now come under our study are due to post-diluvian dispersions.

THE ARK, IN ITS SUCCESSIVE SANCTUA-RIES, A TYPE OF CHRIST IN THE CHURCH IN ALL DISPENSATIONS.

IT is conceded by all scholars who have investigated the question that there was an ante-Sinaitic tabernacle. It is also probable that there was an ante-Sinaitic Ark of the Covenant. The Sinaitic tabernacle, made after the pattern shown Moses in the mount, was set up on the first day of the first month of the second year after the departure of the children of Israel from the land of Egypt. (Ex. xl. 17.) But it is quite evident that there was a tabernacle in the camp of Israel prior to that date. In the third month after leaving Egypt the camp was pitched at the foot of Mount Sinai, and Moses went up into the mount to receive the law and the patterns of the holy things that were to be made. (Ex. xix. 1.) When he descended with the tables of the law in his hands he found the people worshipping the

golden calf that Aaron made during his ab-
sence. We read in Ex. xxxiii. 7 that the next
day after this event, which was long before the
work of making the new tabernacle was begun,
"Moses *took the tabernacle* and pitched it
without the camp, afar off from the camp, and
called it the tabernacle of the congregation.
And it came to pass that every one which
sought the Lord went out unto the tabernacle
which was without the camp." In this we
have proof positive that there was a tabernacle
in the camp of Israel before the Sinaitic tabernacle was made. We go farther back and find
that the Israelites camped in the wilderness of
Sin in the middle of the second month after
leaving Egypt, and there they murmured
against the Lord; and the Lord commanded
Moses "to say unto all the congregation of the
children of Israel, *come near before the Lord;*
for he hath heard your murmurings." It was
then that the Lord sent quails and gave manna
for bread to his people; and at that time
Aaron, as commanded by Moses, filled a golden
pot with manna and "laid it up before the tes-

timony" to be kept for the generations to come. (Ex. xvi. 33, 34.) From this it seems that there was in the ante-Sinaitic tabernacle a holy place for the testimony. And, going still farther back, we find in the history of the transactions of Moses with Pharaoh such expressions as these, "Moses *returned* and came *before the Lord*," and "Moses said *before the Lord*," which certainly imply that there was a certain holy trysting-place, a recognized seat of the divine presence, where God met with Moses, and where he met and communed with his people.

We have already seen that the cherubim and Shechinah, the most significant parts of the Ark of the Covenant, stood just outside of the gate of the garden of Eden, and before them stood the original altar of sacrifice where the fallen race first began to worship.

There is no reason to suppose that the antediluvian fathers were ever deprived of the sacred symbols and types that represented a Saviour to come. It is certain that Noah carried with him into the ark a knowledge of di-

vine worship by sacrifice. One of the very
first things he did on leaving the ark was to
build an altar and to offer sacrifices. (Gen.
viii. 20.) There was doubtless an altar, with its
holy symbols, in the ark itself. This divine
knowledge was transmitted by Noah to those
who came after the flood. The symbols of the
covenant of redemption have always existed
among men, and they may have always been
kept in a sacred tent. If there was not always
a sacred tent, there must have been at least a
sacred and consecrated spot for an altar, and
in connection with it a manifestation of the
Shechinah between the cherubim as a symbol
of the divine presence in the midst of sincere
worshippers. In no age of the world has God
ever left himself without witness on earth.
This is the perpetual testimony—the word that
has been received in all ages as good in the
sight of God our Saviour—that God wills
($\theta \acute{\epsilon} \lambda \epsilon \iota$) that all men should be saved by coming
to a knowledge of the truth, that there is but
one God and one Mediator between God and
men, the Man Christ Jesus, who gave himself a

ransom for all. This is the testimony in all ages—τὸ μαρτύριον καιροῖς ἰδίοις—not a fact *to be* testified in due season, but a truth that has been testified in all its seasons. Jesus Christ is the Saviour of our lost world in the new covenant of redemption, in which mercy, forever harmonized with justice, is enthroned. This is the great truth that was typified and taught in the symbols of worship that were instituted just outside of the gate of the garden of Eden; and those symbols, doubtless, continued to be used in every form of worship unto the days of Moses, always typifying Christ, as he is now preached in the gospel, as the divine and only way of human salvation. This great truth was more fully and clearly typified in the Ark of the Covenant that was made after the divine pattern shown to Moses in the mount, which was, in all its successive sanctuaries, a type of Christ our Saviour, as the one and forever unvarying way of salvation made known in the church in all its dispensations. This teaches the fact that there is but one covenant of redemption, but one Saviour in all ages, and but one church on earth, the church of Christ our Saviour existing in unbroken continuity from the day that man fell unto the final day of the world's complete redemption.

The typical significance of Israel culminated in the temple of Solomon, and terminated with its destruction. The history of the division and of the decline and fall of Israel is not typical. It was, therefore, typically correct for the Ark of the Covenant to disappear with the fall of Solomon's temple. The ark in the Sinaitic tabernacle, where it was kept in the holy of holies, and was seen only by the high priest, and by him only once a year, was a type of Christ our Saviour in the church in the Mosaic dispensation; in the Davidic tabernacle on Mount Zion, where it was always in sight, and accessible to the people without priestly mediation, it was typical of Christ in the present Christian dispensation; and in Solomon's temple, its last dwelling-place on earth, it was typical of Christ our Saviour in the church in the millennial dispensation, which is yet to come.

www.ingramcontent.com/pod-product-compliance
Lightning Source LLC
Chambersburg PA
CBHW021527090426
42739CB00007B/810